YOU'RE SMOKIN' NOW, MR. BUTTS!

Doonesbury Books by G.B. Trudeau

In Large Format

A DOONESBURY BOOK
by G. B. TRUDEAU

YOU'RE SMOKIN' NOW, MR. BUTTS!

SIR, WHAT HAPPENS IF THE PRESIDENT DIES IN COLOMBIA?

I BELIEVE I'D BE SENT TO HIS FUNERAL.

ANDREWS and McMEEL   A UNIVERSAL PRESS SYNDICATE COMPANY   KANSAS CITY • NEW YORK

"Let's pound some duck."

— David Letterman

16

36

46

48

Panel 1: *1999. ABC ANCHORMAN ROLAND HEDLEY CALLS A STAFF MEETING.*

OKAY, WHAT'S THE RUN-DOWN FOR THE SHOW TONIGHT?

WE'VE GOT NINE TAPE PIECES ON DECK, ROLAND...

Panel 2: EIGHT OF THEM ARE DRAMATIZATIONS. WE THOUGHT WE'D LEAD WITH THE BOMBING IN CAIRO. WE'LL BE GETTING LIVE RAW FOOTAGE FROM BURBANK AS SOON AS PROPS CAN MATCH THE CAR...

Panel 3: GOOD. HOW ABOUT THE HURRICANE STORY?

DONE. WE SHOT THE MODEL OF ST. THOMAS THIS A.M.

WE LOST SOME VERISIMILITUDE ON THE LOOTERS. WE ONLY HAD ASIAN MINIATURES IN STOCK.

IS ANYONE BOOKED FOR VICTIM REACTION?

Panel 4: WE'RE READING TIM O'BRIEN AFTER LUNCH. HE'S DONE THREE HURRICANES BEFORE, INCLUDING ETHEL. ALSO SEVERAL FIRES. HE DOES EXCELLENT VICTIM WORK, PROBABLY THE MOST RESPECTED PLAYER IN THE WHOLE NEWS ART DIVISION.

GOOD. ANYTHING ELSE?

Panel 5: YEAH, THE ONE REALITY PIECE IS AN INTERVIEW WITH ROBERT REDFORD ABOUT THE OIL SPILL...

NO WAY! NO ACTOR INTERVIEWS! IT'S NEVER CLEAR WHETHER THEY'RE **BEING** THEMSELVES OR **PLAYING** THEMSELVES!

Panel 6: WHAT IF WE LABEL IT? YOU KNOW, "THIS IS AN ACTUALIZATION."

IT'S A CREDIBILITY THING, MARTY. THIS ISN'T LOCAL NEWS.

OKAY! WHO'S PLAYING ME TONIGHT?

©B Trudeau

61

63

DAY 20.

IT'S A MESS DOWN THERE SIR. WE'RE BASICALLY BUILDING ALL OF PANAMA'S GOVERNING INSTITUTIONS FROM SCRATCH!

WHAT WE URGENTLY NEED IS A CIVILIAN ADMINISTRATOR, SOMEONE ON THE GROUND WHO CAN DIRECT THE RECONSTRUCTION OF THE COUNTRY!

GOT ANYONE IN MIND?

YES, SIR. A RETIRED FOREIGN SERVICE OFFICER WITH GOOD COLONIAL EXPERIENCE. HE'LL DO IT IF WE CAN SETTLE ON A TITLE.

OKAY, HOW ABOUT "MAXIMUM PROCONSUL"?

DONE! FAX MY CONTRACT TO SOUTHERN COMMAND!

SORRY, DUKE, I CAN'T SPARE YOU. I'M GONNA HOLD YOU TO YOUR CONTRACT!

BUT MR. T, THIS APPOINTMENT TO PANAMA IS A **MAJOR** OPPORTUNITY...

PANAMA CITY IS THE NEXT HAVANA, THE NEXT SAIGON! IT'S WIDE OPEN, AND AS PROCONSUL, I'LL BE MAKING THE DECISIONS ON DEVELOPMENT— HOUSING, HOTELS, CASINOS, THE WORKS!

DON'T BE A STRANGER.

AYE, AYE, SIR!

SIR, MAY I BE THE FIRST TO CONGRATULATE YOU ON YOUR APPOINTMENT TO MAXIMUM PROCONSUL OF PANAMA. I ONLY WISH I COULD JOIN YOU!

UNFORTUNATELY, SINCE OUR DIVORCE, I'VE DEVELOPED ROOTS AND COMMITMENTS RIGHT HERE IN NEW JERSEY. I HAVE A NICE HOME THAT I'VE JUST DECORATED...

...AND I HAVE TWO CATS AND FOUR PLANTS THAT NEED ME. I ALSO HAVE A JOB I LOVE, FOR WHICH I AM BOTH APPRECIATED AND WELL-COMPENSATED!

WHAT A SHAME. I NEED SOMEONE TO TASTE MY FOOD.

I'LL GO PACK.

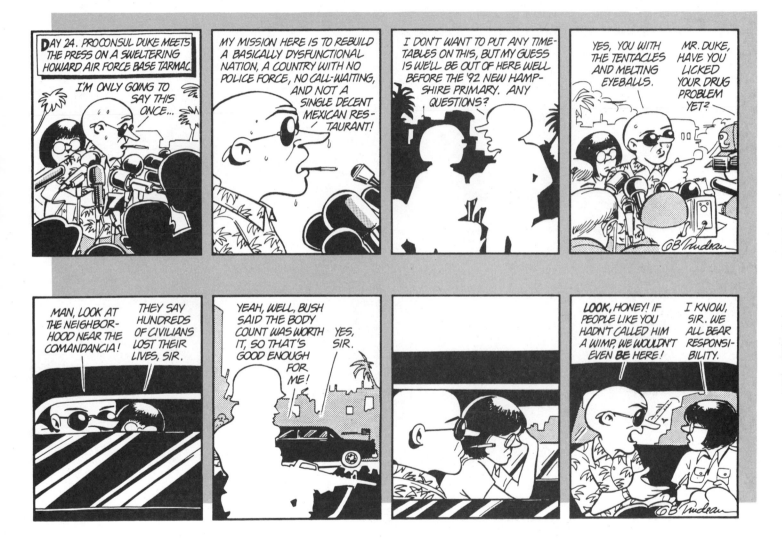

MARVELOUS MARC'S KONUNDRUM KORNER 'GO FIGURE!'

KIDS! HERE'S A REAL **BRAIN-TEASER!** TRY DISPOSING OF TODAY'S COMIX SECTION WITHOUT VIOLATING GEORGE BUSH'S PROPOSED CONSTITUTIONAL AMENDMENT ON FLAG DESECRATION! SURE, THIS FLAG'S ONLY PAPER, BUT IT'S STILL OUR **NATION'S SYMBOL!**

REMEMBER:
▶ NO USING IT TO LINE A BIRD CAGE OR TRAIN A PUPPY—THAT'S **DESECRATION!**
▶ NO THROWING IT IN THE GARBAGE—DITTO!
▶ NO USING IT TO START A FIRE IN THE FIREPLACE— THAT'S **FLAG BURNING!**

GOOD LUCK!

SOLUTION ON FAR RIGHT.

SOLUTION? THERE **IS** NONE! YOU'RE STUCK WITH THIS FLAG UNTIL IT CRUMBLES! SORRY, KIDS, BUT THAT'S THE WAY IT GOES SOMETIMES IN.... KONUNDRUM KORNER!

GBTrudeau